Michael R. Collings

NAKED TO THE SUN:

· ·

Dark Visions of Apocalypse

BORGO PRESS / WILDSIDE PRESS

www.wildsidepress.com

ı

Poems in this collection have appeared (frequently in different versions) in the following:

Aliens and Lovers, 1983: "Orchisophilia," "Aube" ["Alien Vistas" IV]. Approaching Critical Mass (in press): "Critical Mass," "The Last Pastoral," "The Meeting on the Edge of Eternity." Bulletin, Bay Area Poets Coalition: "Hungry, the Ocean." California State Poetry Quarterly: "Sonata Enigmata." Dialogue: "Summer, 1953." Expressionists (Pepperdine University): "The Burning," "The Children's Merry-Go-Round," "Summer, 1953." Fantasy Book: "The Sorceress of the Silvered Wood." Mythellany: "From the Womb of the World." Owlflight: "Alien Vistas," "Return to Avalon," "My Last Nemesis" (accepted but unpublished), "Wiros" (accepted but unpublished). Our Twentieth Century's Greatest Poems, 1982: "Sea Swells." The San Fernando Poetry Journal: "The Blood Burns," "The Meadow Yesterday," "Earth Mother," "Migration." Space & Time: "Mythmaker," "Three Songs from Dracula." Star*Line [Science Fiction Poetry Association]: "The Dark is Deep," "Eternity Has Finally Died," "Fifth Movement and Final," "Migration," "One With Him," "Rydra Wong: A Quotella," "Visions." Velocities: "Naked to the Sun"

Michael R. Collings has published one previous collection of poetry, A Season of Calm Weather (1974) and scores of individual poems in magazines and journals. He is currently Poetry Editor for Dialogue. Wearing another hat, Dr. Collings is a professor in the Humanities Division at Pepperdine University and has written a series of critical studies of Stephen King for Starmont House.

For Brian W. Aldiss,

David Gerrold,

The Science Fiction Poetry Association,

and Ted Dikty of Starmont House . . .

and Judi, _sine qua non_

Library of Congress Cataloging-in-Publication Data

Collings, Michael R.
    Naked to the sun.

    I. Title.
PS3553.Ó474696N3   1986   821'.914   85-30248
ISBN 0-930261-77-1   -
ISBN 0-930261-76-3 (pbk.)

Table of Contents

IV. APOCALYPSE AND BEYOND

NAKED TO THE SUN (I)

Naked to the sun
when we transplanted it in May,
the apple tree crisped in the August sun.

Leaves crumbled from arthritic petioles,
Flaked into drifts like golden snow
To hide Bermuda grass.

By November, it stood bare,
Waiting beneath a fading sun
And casting spider shadows on the earth,

Waiting . . .
for discovery
and change.

I.

The World and Time

Summer, 1953

I was six.
I wheeled Grandpa's milk cans out
to wait like patient soldiers for the cheese truck.
I strutted in a new red and blue
corduroy cowboy suit.

(Korea was over.)

I raided raspberries,
squishing succulence on my tongue.
I slaughtered alfalfa-straw snakes in overgrown
        fields.
I rode stick horses at full gallop
across the log bridge, risking tumbles
into nettles and polliwog slime.

(Viet Nam was about to begin.)

I fished for six-inch whoppers.
I slept out on a rusty spring,
waking when a 1940s Ford or Chevy
or Nash crunched the gravelled road.
I stared at stars, my eyes not yet myopic enough
to need corrective lenses.

(Sputnik was an engineer's conception.)

I rode with Grandpa to deliver eggs,
flats of eggs on the back seat,
warm-stuffy grey seat-pile in front,
a green translucent spinner on the wheel.
Four hours into Burley and back--
ninety miles.

(The moon rose untouched.)

MY GRANDMOTHER, DYING

settles into rusty cushions.
The faded armchair enfolds her
in velvet pile

worn thin. Dying slowly
she touches a peacock
crocheted in blue

and gold--once dowry,
now rosary of memories.
Thick fingers

tremble, touch
intricate webwork
knots. Eyes

cloud silver-blue, tearless.
Behind clouds
once billowed

light. Now veins
and nerves and
flesh web

the glow alive. Life
threads weave outward
from the

cooling core, passing
being and
beyond.

But now, settled
in rusty cushions,
she fingers fraying knots.

Soon the peacock pattern
will unravel beyond
repair, and light

spill outward uncontrolled
leaving darkened fingers poised over
emptiness

THE LAST ROSE

For Eva Hurd

The last rose shimmers
in autumn.
It bloomed scarlet once, or
crimson--deeper
and red with red beyond
blood. Now the petals
crust and blacken.
Velvet nap clots smooth
shallowness. White
tears at the base where
petals wedded withered calyx.

The others are dead,
scattered motes of wrinkled red
spinning in the air
or swollen wombs stained
orange by first frost.
One lives, one memory
and foreshadowing.

There. The petals drop.
Fragrance scatters ash
upon its gravestone.

BETRAYAL

They told me my cougar was only a silly child's
    dream;
They told me so--and so--but I had seen
It purring in grey rocks that grew beyond the
    aspens
And had rushed back, faint from breath held in
    suspense,
To warn them all. "Child," my grandmother had said,
"There are no cougars here. They are all dead,
Or hidden high above the snow-line in close caves.
    No alarms
Have rung for years down here, close by the farms."

They told me he would heal, that his red blood
Staining rusty flagstones would wash away, would
    flood
Away as soon as Grandpa sluiced the stones
With water cloudy as memories of old bones
From the irrigation ditch across the lawn. Grandma
    stoked
The cast-iron stove, boiling water while they broke
(Or tried to break) his fever. Grandma made my bed
In the attic. In the morning he was dead.

They told me that the park was safe--that I could
    run
there on my way to meet him as the sun
Sank red. I saw him coming . . . and from the
    brush
Head-high beside me, a German shepherd in a rush
Exploded. My father yelled. The dog fled
Yipping like a thing in agony. He caught my red,
Red blood in a paper soda-carton (irrational,
    insane),
But all I saw was redness and the black, black
    pain.

A DEATH IN HAMBURG

Head braced on a book,
A word-book to keep the jaws
Closed. No words spill
Spilling silence
Black snow hurrying
Flurrying
Slipping beneath the door

Bare walls, bare floor
Bare bulb--white light
On a sheet like snow
Hair like snow
Flesh like snow

Outside the door
Damp and cold
Doors into blackness
The closed door opens
Spilling white light into the halls

THE MEADOW YESTERDAY

The meadow yesterday
today is dry and brown
bare earth

worth more than many men´s
dreams when transformed
into structures

rupturing the landscape
thrusting skyward.
Snake and rabbit

habitually at home in soil
creep dispossessed like dwindling
·shadows--

Meadows die. Snakes and rabbits
die that we might be
possessors.

HUNGRY, THE OCEAN

Hungry, the ocean
eats warm sand
beneath my feet and

drinks dampness
crusting on my legs.
I taste of salt, as

if preparing for the twilight
meal. And the archaic ocean
re-ingests

elements
once quiescent
in its womb.

DAMP SAND STREAKS

damp sand streaks
blood
grey glittering blood
along his thigh

gulls skitter
cormorants perch vulture-like
on rock cliffs bleached
with excrement

crabs sidle forward
tear strands of flesh
and waves wipe
sand to let the blood run red

FIRE DANCER

To the **tik-tik-tik** of a hollow log
heart-thrum rumbling
flickering night,

the dancer rose, silver-gold
gleaming fingers of
flame weaving
darkness into light.

Faster. Louder the log
trembles.
The Fire Dancer,
one with heat and light,

presses the chill.
silence grows--the Fire Dancer
rises, passions knotting limbs
like ocean-fire. And the flames

recede. The Fire Dancer
drops as the log falls silent.
In the vacancies between far stars
the fire dancer returns to coals

and finally to ash.

THE CHILDREN´S MERRY-GO-ROUND

The children´s merry-go-round
pie-segmented kaleidoscoping in the park

flushed cheeks and
screams that cut
through lightning air

sunburned shoulders
T-shirts flaring flames
in a whirlwind

blood scorching my back
running rivers beneath my waistband
Beneath the pain I remember

hot blood
on my back, bolts
and screwheads painted red

kaleidoscoping on the children´s merry-go-round
in the park

EARTH MOTHER

From the plane
granite looms above brown folds
smooth and worn
like ruminant molars
dulled with chewing
against the edge of Time.

TRIGGER IN THE MIND

I killed my father. I was a child
Then, wild and well-full of fears
And tears that boiled behind slit eyes
Like water rising to crush--brutally--
Concrete walls. The dam might burst--

It should--it hadn´t then--I was a child,
Thirteen, that´s all. The rifle hung
On a rung above the dark oak mantleboard,
A hoard of memories and warnings
Till warming in my wrath I fired . . . .

There was no shot. My father lives.
He gives my children cap-gun pistols
On their birthdays--fishes, hunts
With them. And yet--when I was thirteen,
A child no more, I stretched
And killed my father.

SPUTNIK

Evening.
Montana evening.
Cool and black, the memory
Of a grave.
I remember silence.

With four kids, our home
Must have been noisy.

But I remember silence,
Chill, and blackness,
Looking up at stars
No more my own. **They** had caught up,
Surpassed--they were there.
And the stars burned black
In that long Montana night.

ORION

The stars, once diamond-dust
Trails from exploding crystal balls,
Glow dimmer now.

Orion marched ponderously
Beneath an Idaho sky. I woke,
My sleeping bag saturated with dew,
My feet chilled, crickets echoing
From alfalfa fields.
I thought I knew the future,
And Orion marched on ponderously.

Last night, I searched for him.
Armed with volumes on astronomy, I stared
Through the glare of an LA sky.
I found Orion, of course. It wasn't hard.
It took a flashlight and two books--
Ten minutes to trace hypothetical lines,
And a moment more to see through
Joints and sinews into distances.

Suns burn in vacuum. The diamond dust
Tarnished. And Orion merely stars.

II

In the Shadow of the Gods

CURLING SOUTHWARD, ICE-WINDS CALL

Curling southward, ice-winds call
raucously, geese silhouetting waning light,
faint foreshadowings of fall.

Tattered leaves cartwheel, swirl
in muted browns, while through the night,
curling southward, ice-winds call.

Pumpkin clusters, corn shocks canting tall
against the sunset--images of delight
and faint foreshadowings of fall.

Denuded oaks, distorted branches gall-
infested, bracket summer hope-flight,
curling southward. Ice-winds call

like banshees as frost-killed apples scrawl
decaying patterns of dusty blight,
faint foreshadowings of the Fall.

And the brown-brittle rose garden, wall
in ruins, fades into frosted night.
Curling southward, ice-winds call,
faint remembrances of the Fall.

GOD, LIKE A GREAT GREY UNCLE

God, like a great grey uncle,
looms outside our lives,
gold watch-chain spanning
pinstripe vest, hands
jammed in pockets stretched
by pounds and years.

He intrudes on occasion--
Christmas and Easter
usually. We dress up
and slick down rebellious hair
and polish shoes against uncreased
trousers, hoping to convince him

we love him truly, yes we do,
and please don't bother to revise your will.

EXPECTO RESURRECTIONEM

Silvered beads
Skim shining hemp. Black eaves
Weep a single bead
Striking center.
And the row slips
One by One
Into spreading grapevine leaves.
All summer they will wait
Invisible
until
September strips green
From swollen purpled beads
Clustering spring-rain sweet
And ripe.

Ad Astra PerFidem

The totem of their god was marred:
Stigmata starred its palms, and wrists,
And feet. The Elder waited patiently,
While through wrenched teeth I hissed

As

If a single questing sound. He spoke:
"Not us, not here. Another world,
In darkness dressed"--he broke
A curious thrumming sound. "Another people

One

Has told us of." I swallowed stone
And would not speak. "Another world
Where angles dwelt, where droned
That hideous strength against our God,

Who

Straightened him that first had warred
To bend all life beneath infinity.
A world of stupid men, bored
With life, experimenting with

Sin

As if they knew not what would come
Of it." I looked around. A world
Like mine, unlike my distant home
In never having suffered war

And

Futile strife. A world where God
Had come--one time, in glory-light--
And spoken thoughts which blossomed awe
And echo, though their legends

Fault

Frail history. They waited One.
He came.

                    That was all.
                                That simple.
          That wonder-full. Here, on the rim
          Of man´s extension into space,

Has

          Man (on the first habitable earth)
          Found humanoids like us,
          Enough like to be brothers. Birth
          Of a new universe! Yet spirit-death

Overcame

          Our pretentions. For the God
          and Lord of Worlds innumerable
          Was here. And on the planet where I trod
          As child . . . only there, on one

Home

          In all the Universe, did man--
          God´s progeny--crucify
          And scourge His Son. Our simple plan,
          To proselyte for humankind,

Seek

          Equals on the seedling planets far,
          Is come to nothing--ashes heaped
          Upon our pride. And so we leave this star,
          Return to Earth, the only world

We

          Know to kill a Christ.
          The only needing desperately
          His birth with us as man--the price
          To cauterize our weeping hearts

Now.

CELEBRATION

On that night--
that night of all solemn nights--
a thousand million faces
blossomed skyward
like moonflowers (silvered
by the light of one moon,
touched with shadow by the second),
eye-trajectories
to The Wing.

In worship, yes; but not
in dark idolatry.
The Wing held no sacred hopes itself;
its arc of stars
pinioned planets opening
through other quadrants of their galaxy.

They could count the Twelve Suns
and see the darkness
just beneath The Wing--
darkness where, when the night
was still, just so, and eyes
squinted to tight lines
crossing faces lost in awe--
then, perhaps, one in a thousand
could see the blot of light
that was The Galaxy.

And on that night,
a thousand million faces
celebrated
The Coming on a distant world,
too many thousand years ago to count--
The Coming
and an End.

Each dweller on the planet,
each on myriads of whirling worlds,
knew of Him, spoke of Him,
saw Him.

But on this night, with faces glowing as
bright buds
and eyes like slits of deep black faith,

they saw--perhaps--a smudge that was
The Galaxy bearing hidden in its womb

the yellow star
that saw Him born.

THE BLOOD BURNS

The blood burns--
Gods! I had thought blood cold
but it burns down my side
between fingers once mine clutching
at my wound.

The blood burns--
stripes of flame
growing from a tremor in my breath.
I ran once from threads of flame,
from quaking earth.
Ran, and hid myself in shadowy groves
and saw . . . .

the blood burns
where I touched the corpse accidentally
before the stone rolled
across its opening. Then,
my fingers froze with the chill of death.

But now . . . .

the blood burns
and I dwindle to a hidden spark
and the blood burns no more.
My enemies exult at my death,
a fallen warrior.
The blood slows, crusts brown
upon the soil.

And there is nothing--
save the sound of sandstone rolling over
sun-parched earth.

THE MEETING ON THE EDGE OF ETERNITY

I met him at the cross
roads, in a desert flat
just out of Reno. A chance
meeting poignant with the loss

of a vision. Wastelands stretched matte
grey, a blessed relief, no dance
of afterburn assaulted eyes
day after day. He sat

mesquite shaded He heard me pant
in the noon shimmer-heat. Flies
haloed his greying hair (the first
living things, other than himself), enhanced

his other-worldliness. he squatted on a rise,
three-shrub-crowned, watching a valley cursed
by fatal closeness to humankind.
Mouth drier than thirst, cries

more feral than polite, I burst
into a run, scuttled up the gravel rind
of the skull-smooth hill, tripped on a
coyote corpse, and nursed

a throbbing kneecap as I climbed
the final grade, stopped dead still,
and tried to resurrect my unused voice.
Here was a second of my world-lost kind.

What could I say? The pill
of shame cut acid-bitter. Moist
lips quivered but would not speak. We
stared, he and I, until the evening chill

settled wraithy over the waste
and on blue radiation-silhouetted peaks
thrusting turquoise fires into the north.
We had made our choice,

his people, mine . . . choosing in weak
unwisdom. And our species´ worth
was measured in that freedom. I waited,
hoped and feared that he would speak

to me, the last, together at the birth
of loneliness. Darkness mated
with the livid blue of death,
and I heard him laugh--not mirth

but agony. The sound grated
to a ragged sand-screed breath
and died. In its place
a murmur muted

to a sigh: "Life, not death,
was my intent." His face
glowed, transfigured in the light,
unearthly, passionless in Passion, bereft

of all emotion. His pace
increased. The tight,
tense voice wove words again: "As a hen
her chicks, so would I give you place

beneath my wing." His eyes breathed bright,
as bright almost as the wide-irradiated fen
of nothingness in the distant north. I glared
into fast-drawing night

and wept--for myself, for the worlds of men.
I had alone survived, I thought--to be paired
with . . . . But no one sat beneath the
      skull-shade tree.

I stood alone, the last, and I despaired.

ONE WITH HIM

" . . . what we regard as the flow of time in fact
moves in the opposite direction to its apparent
one . . . . Energy accumulates from less organized
to more highly organized bodies: piles of rust can
integrate into iron rods."

--Brian W. Aldiss, Cryptozoic!

Immortal Christ wraithes through
Eastern twilight, entering
The Cave of Birth. Cold flesh
Awaits agony and birth upon the Cross--
Birth remembered by prophets
Through the future to Adam's time.
　　　Three days flee--sunrise on Friday
Evening. Spirit invests waiting
Flesh. Shattered legs knit; blood
Spurts blindness from the soldier's eye--
Ascends the wooden shaft to thrust
Warmth into Christ's pale breast and
Make whole a broken heart.
　　　Time moves: suffering of trial,
Betrayal's pain, glory in Jerusalem,
Wonder of discipleship--arriving
At peaceful death in the stable.
The God-child returns to his mother
And his God.
　　　Eons wander--humanity assembles.
Demons sweltering in Milton's Hell
Surge into Heaven, gradually forget
Rebellious thought until at last
Christ and Lucifer meet--and Lucifer
Restored.
　　　Civil warfare forgotten,
And at the End, all children
Of the great immortal God
Gather unto him
Eternal and unchanging.
　　　The plan fulfilled.
Creation gathered at the foot
Of God--and none are lost,
And none are left behind.

THE BURNING

Smoke from Cortes´ ships
Rises dark as mourning wings
Against grey-silver. The sun slips
Into night. In clotted rings

Flame-shadowed strangers crouch alone
To face exotic Gods.   As night
Knits webwork carvings on high stone
Pyramids, the smoke (light

Now, tinged with crimson) curls,
Twists into strange faces,
Forms obliquely familiar, swirls
Best suited to the Sacred Places:

Quetzalcoatl, white-edged tear
Of smoke; Texcatlipoca--high
Deities of a dying land. Near
Evening Star, golden embers fly
Heavenward. Perhaps the gods appear
Only when they are about to die.

III

Nightmares in Daytime

THE DARK IS DEEP

Shades like ghosts caress the lawn;
Wild winds chill and yew trees moan.
The dark is deep, falling to dawn.

Headstones glimmer in a yawn
Of broken teeth. In death's head zone
The dark is deep, paling to dawn.

A moonlight scimitar slices upon
winks of ivory, glistens of bone:
The dark is deep, paling to dawn.

The dead arise, traverse the lawn;
Cerements flutter, slack jaws groan.
The dark is deep, falling to dawn.

They circle slowly; empty graves yawn
Wide to me, splitting the loam--
the dark is deep, calling to dawn.

They wreathe me, wraithy bones upon
My flesh, and pull. I scream. I moan.
The dark is deeper, failing the dawn.

WIROS

Here shadowed
from seering sun
this body seems mine almost--
or I its, I do not

know. I run, the knife in my heart
matching the knife in my hand.
Blood streams naked thighs
flashing red as I

run--hot red from my kill,
terrifying, attracting.
Within shadows my quarry
cowers. It knows I am

here, not who or what.
It fears the phantom-
shadow of day,
killing and

killing. By night they search
but will not, cannot find
or know I am with them
as they search, am

the monster--and in darkness
I will not know it either. Now
I run, naked in sunset, bleeding
from thorns and briars, heart

hammered by the demon I am
become--hideous body erect,
hairless, clawless, fangless, slaying
brothers. I weep

to die, but cannot. Day-
nightmare, at night oblivion
of reality. With the night
I will become a wolf again.

MY LAST NEMESIS

There he stands, as if alive
glowering down, baleful eyes and
scimitar smile. I have hung him
in the study to remind me,
to remind me always of my
danger--and of yours, my child. So
long now he has hunted me, as
if he did not understand my
immortality. I keep him
there, gilt-framed and painted by this
hand--eternal life has its
rewards, you know.
                    Who is it, do
you ask? My foolish child, there stands the
enemy, Von Helsing in the
flesh (or in the oils, rather).
My nemesis and yours.
                    Speak up;
what's that? He's dead, you say? I
don't believe it . . . . A century?
That's the reason I've not seen him
poking after shadows, strewing
magic wafers in my earth.
                    Ah,
well, he hangs there still in oils,
nemesis, murderer, stalker
in the day. Mark him well, my
child, shun . . . .
                    Of course I heard.
Yes, he's dead. And I'm not senile
Yet, nor ever am to be. Listen
well, my child.   I've lived long years now,
And I know, my foolish child, their
searching, killing, prying kind is
just as lasting as our own.
There's always a Von Helsing.

37

THREE SONGS FROM <u>DRACULA</u>

I. A Threnody of Wolves

How they howl, yowl, growl
on icy winds--
in the turret a white face glows
discorporate dust
spinning corporality.

And they howl.

Living death feeds
on living blood.

And they yowl.

Inn-doors bolted, lanterns lit
but shaded by the shadow
from the castle turret.

And they growl.

With human tongues cry
tears of immortal death,
anguish quilted night
and echo across sleigh-runner tracks.

And they growl, yowl, howl.

II. Renfield´s Litany, As Overheard
By Professor Von Helsing

O lord of night and darkness´ flight,
Master of death and fear--
From far and near, grant me ear,
And send me death . . .
                              To Life!

Skulking rats and chittering bats
Fill corners of my cell--
Though in dark Hell I feed quite well

38

On bones and bloody breath . . .
                    To Life!

Roaches race and webworks lace
While day's sharp light soon dies--
And spiders' eyes and tasty flies
Are swallowed in a breath . . .
                    To Life!

O somber chill, dread silent still--
But wait! Melt back, stone walls!
For in the halls my Master calls
And bids me come through death . . .
                    To Life!

III. The Bloofer Lady

White lady
Light lady
Like a sunbeam shimmer shadow--
Gauzy garments
Floating filaments
Fingers long and slim and
Sharp
Curve toward my heart.

White lady
Night lady
Like a shadow's shadow dimming--
Scarlet eyes
Undead cries
Teeth long and slim and
Sharp
Smile toward my neck.

SECRET SHADOW

It's here. I feel it crouching in cold night
Behind my door. It waits its own
Still time to tendril out
And touch my toes.
I shiver and groan

As darkness settles like a shadow-blight
On fields. It catches breath--a bone
Of blackness in night's throat;
It rolls and grows--
A murmured moan

Roils my lips, spreading moth-soft fright
On wings of shade. It swells a dome
Of darkness. I breathe great gouts
Of fear. It knows!
I reach . . . am thrown

Against my pillow. I scream as somewhere light
Blinds night. My door flung open. A cone
Of pain whirls dark in a rout.
I curse my foes
and cry, alone.

Eternally
Alone.

THE SORCERESS OF THE SILVERED WOOD

"Who enters my wood with booted foot
Shall find but filth and dross;
His breath shall not lighten--his song shall lie
    mute
While he treads my paths of moss."

    And while he crept,
    The sorceress slept
    And silently wept her loss.

"Who enters my wood with horse and cart
Shall find but rutted trails;
The magic of iron shall slash my green heart
And pierce my loam with nails."

    And in wild glade
    The sorceress´ shade
    Impatiently fades through vales.

"Who enters my wood with sword and shield
Shall know but blood and pain:
His bare bones shall bleach, his flesh lie
    congealed
Like moss after winter´s foul rain."

    She felt his ache
    Like an ashen stake,
    And wept to forsake him again.

"But he who enters with naked arm,
With naked foot and breast
Thus braves the Perilous Realm--no harm
To him, but golden rest;

"For I shall wed the one who comes
To court me in silvered woods:
And I shall grant him his heart´s own home
And pledge with my maidenhood."

    She plaited her hair
    With her crystal tear,
    And whispered to where he stood
    In the heart of the Silvered Wood.

THE WIND FROM WHIRL-AWAY

It rose at dusk, a demon wind
That swirled around grey eaves.
Across the plain still damp with rain
It fluttered fragile leaves.

Asleep that night we did not know
What blew that devil's breath.
Warm in our homes we felt its moans . . .
And dreamed of crimson death.

We did not see the eldritch glow
That fingered distant hills--
Nor how it ran on poisoned sand
To pulse beyond our sills.

By dawn it spun a dizzing whirl.
The stoutest branches swayed.
And when we woke, we breathed to choke
On dust from Whirl-Away.

It flickered frozen in stale rooms.
It stung with whispered cold.
The morning light, once sun-gold bright,
Shone green-tinged, as with mold.

By noon it wrenched rough breath from lips
Crusted with salty blood.
Infants wailed. Red roof-tiles flailed
Like sea-crests at full flood.

"The Wizard-Witch," the whispers wept,
"That stranger and his curse"--
Soft spoken fears like brittle spears
Transfixed our hearts . . . and worse,

The wind now seethed with sentient strength
And battered mud-caked walls.
For a stranger's thirst we feared the worst,
And trembled in dank halls.

It raged all day. At dusk one man
Dared face its ravenous lash.
It pinned him there in the village square
And flayed his bones of flesh.

The air grew thick with murky blood.
We smelled the stench of death.
With icy bowels we heard the howls
Of the winds as they died to breath.

In the sudden hush the Wizard walked
Like Death beside its bier.
He took one sip from the well's smooth lip--
None saw him disappear.

But his croaking laughter cuts our ears.
Our fingers slowly clenched.
"Oh, did you think the wind would drink
Your water, and be quenched?

"None but blood can salve that thirst"--
And with the dying day,
We heard his last as his whisper passed--
The Wizard of Whirl-Away.

"Poor old fellow!"

"Demented, probably. At least
that's what I thought when I first ·saw him
straddling the beach, dressed up
like a child at a costume ball."

"I wonder where he came from.
It couldn't have been far;
that armor weighed enough to make
it difficult to walk. Perhaps he came
from some nearby asylum, or a home
where relatives and friends have humored him
in his delusions. That seems cruel,
encouraging an old man's madness so,
and dressing him in dusty, dinted mail;
but maybe not, since he seemed quaintly pleased
and harmless in his vagaries. He might
have come from nowhere, though, so quietly
he moved upon the beach. It was a shock
to see him standing there . . . ."

" . . . . Brandishing that rusty sword
with cut-glass on the hilt,
green and red stones set in faded gilt,
calling it <u>Excaliburn</u>, or some such name,
and mumbling wildly of the sea,
of death, and of a lady in a lake.
Not here, and that's the truth! The only lake
for miles is Barrow's Slough, that pit
of sludge and slime where urchins hunt frogs
in rotting mud and ragged reeds.
A lady living there would be a sight,
dressed in dripping, slimy mold, with
rottenness for her perfume, putrescent
logs for throne of state."

"Ha! You paint no pretty portrait, friend.
He must be daft--but still I wonder how he came
so close unheard. I could have sworn no soul
but us was on the beach--and then we turned
toward the sea and there he was, alone.
I didn't even notice any prints,
no footsteps in the sand. It's weird,

unnatural."

"Unnatural? No,
just some old fellow prating of knights
and kings and battlements. He probably
stood too close to hot artillery
in the war and hasn´t been quite right since."

"I guess that´s true. He mumbled badly--
or his speech was impaired, I don´t know which.
Anyway, his words were hard to understand. I wish
I knew where he has gone. That´s as strange
as anything. One moment there--then not,
leaving behind the smell of mouldy earth.
He murmured something--"The time is not yet
      come"--
Or some like nonsense, if I heard him right."

"And something more about an "oval lion,"
whatever that might be."

"And when I turned to you
and back again, he was not there.
Where he had been, just dry sand."

"Wait. What´s this? A piece of greenish glass.
It must have shaken from his sword as he
brandished it. Cheap glass--I probably
should leave it here. Some boy will pass
playing pirate-voyage and will chance
upon this ´precious jewel´--it is well made,
      though,
much better than I thought, and clear.
It has such depth, as if it were a pool
of green-flamed fire. Do you think . . . ?"

"Be serious! Surely you can´t believe
it is an emerald. That big! It would
be worth the treasure of a king
if it were real."

"Perhaps . . . but still I think
I´ll keep it for a while. Perhaps to help
remember that old man. Look, can you see that?
Out there, beneath the setting sun, where waves
seem liquid gold, a gleaming highway

45

to the West.   Is that a ship, that distant spot?
I think I see three naked masts,
naked to the sun; but no,
the currents there are not that strong.
The gold has faded green again,
and now the sun is gone."

"There was no ship!   You see too many things
that are not there.
Let´s go.
I´ll let you treat me to a beer."

MINOTAUR

Through labyrinthine NewYorkLos
AngelesChicago weaves
Beastman/Manbeast
Sexual
Hunger feeds
Pain with pain

She walks highheeled
knitting shadow to shadow
with threads of passing
knitting moment to moment.
She falters beneath a streetlamp
soiled globe spilling sparse light
that barely shadows.
She falters, looks back, clutches
purple sequined purse
and slips into shadow
and screams

Pain for pain he
Feeds hunger, sates
Sexuality
Manbeast--head and genitalia
Of man, heart of beast,
Soul of beast
Unravelling patterns in Los
AngelesChicago
Labyrinthine NewYork.

FROM THE WOMB OF THE WORLD

From the womb of the world whispers a moan
As the atmosphere shivers, silently slain,
And the last of the High Elves lingers alone.

Through lead-coffered heavens, rose-clouds blown
Like derelicts scuttle for fear of the rain--
From the womb of the world whispers a moan.

And a fire-ball spreading-out filagrees cones
On a mountain range, thrumming a legend's refrain
Where the last of the High Elves lingers alone.

Ashen evergreens, needleless Norns, like bone
Thrown on cinder-heaps twisting arthritic in pain;
From the womb of the world whispers a moan.

And brown silicon soil melts glass-down:
Fertile imaginings struggle in vain,
And the last of the High Elves lingers alone.

With the last human impulse, the last man alone
Faults fantasy worlds. He dies, and they wane.
From the womb of the world whispers a moan,
And the last of the High Elves lingers . . . is
      gone.

IV

Apocalypse and Beyond

MYTHMAKER

I stood officiously on the plank decking
of an oil-barrel raft, one of thirty
khaki-clad Boy Scouts, as I

pinioned constellations with my four-cell
flash. Cepheus bowed at my words,
Scorpio arched poison-

drawn and impotent light-centuries
away. I spoke off-handedly
of giant Deneb fifteen

hundred light-years from
Old Sol, never comprehending
just how far ahead a light year

twines. I spoke, pinioning constellations,
a primitive, poised on sodden rocks
(sharpened shafts spearing

eastward-spawning salmon)
unaware of salty universes
unimaginably beyond my tribal stream.

Now, I weave wordnets and spread new worlds
like captive butterflies,
wings extended, held

by hair-thin pins below each vein,
scales shimmering, secret
hues exposed and no more

secret. Tales beyond truth--exotics
spread on balsa-board--stories
soar beyond this earth to galaxies unknown.

Yet I remain the Indian, plunging spears
into vaporous streams, hoping
to find words and worlds

as far beyond my own as salmon spawning
grounds beyond the sea, or as the
caterpillar differs

from the Monarch hovering
on tissue air. Maker of myth,
seeker of worlds, I write.

VISIONS

A thick red volume on the velvet shelf,
awesomely foreboding.

And as I read:

        a rose-red glistening inlines
        arms cocked rifle-tense
        (rifle unencountered yet)
        arms strained forward
        shoulders a taut-stringed
        (also unencountered)
        bow.

        A boomerang spin-whistling
        whirrs the speed of thought
        arching dawn-bronze deserts
        unimaginable
        then descending,

        returns to present
        narrowness
        thud-slapping its maker's palm

        unchanged

outwardly
yet inwardly altered by
time-vague hints
of opal sands.

RYDRA WONG: A Quotella

"For the root is the dream. And the translator is
the God."

--Ursula K. Le Guin, <u>The</u>
<u>Word for World is Forest</u>

For truth I breathed a filtered air, for that
The poems blossom strangely in a stranger land; at
Root of both, immune from cutworm ravages,
Is . . . no, swirls (<u>is</u> is mere passivity)
The ineffable nebulous, the
Dream-defining of undreamable otherness.
And the poet-<u>vates</u> self-anointed,
The mediator of yet unacquainted worlds,
Translator of unknowables into emerald images
Is (<u>I</u>-passive, state of being, static vessel)

The abyss where valanced reality gapes,
God-wanderer, maker-pilgrim in alienscapes.

ORCHISOPHILIA

The first men walk through
dense unEarthly growth.

Between pseudobulbs
a fleshy stalk
thickens, lengthens--
a hooded bulb of green
thrusts sunward
among curling sword-leaves.
The hood pulls back.
One by one
buds twist
swell
burst a spray
of creamy blooms--
microscopic seed
filtering through
air-not-air.

The first men walk through
dense unEarthly growth
and are men no more.

BENEATH THE BLUE SUN

Low in the (<u>by definition</u>) west
(<u>because of sunfall there</u>)
lapis lazuli
plucks sleepily
at the planet´s amber skirt.

Viscid waves tower
spinnacles to an oblate moon
hunching through a star-stained universe.
Coarse gravel hides beneath
pacific swells.

Not far away (if men could mount the air
and half-jump/fly like Terran insects
leaf to quivering leaf) forests loom
dark, foreboding,
branches twisting gracefully

like dancers´ finger-threads
of violet.
Somewhere in the darkness, beings
breathe sibilant sleep,
dream alien dreams

as a blunt-nosed <u>something</u>
glows through dying light
screes downward, slicing
the squat moon´s arc, chording
the blue sun´s sphere
and lands, blunt nose buried in a copse
of moss.

Its glowing dies, metals
(on a metalless world) cool
into pregnant night.
Wavelets
hiss-withdraw,
scurry beneath inquisitive sister-swells
racing toward the shore.

Night passes.
Light spills above eastern
(<u>because of sunrise there</u>)
dark in turquoise coronets.

A scrannel grating--
ssssssts of oxygen
poisoning the atmosphere.

The ship ejects slick-silver forms,
bilaterally symmetrical, quadrupedal,
crowned with sheening inflorescences.
They cluster, separate--some
toward the womb-warm seas,

others to shadowed undergrowth now silent,
wary-alert as nightdreams fade,
sleep flees sapphire day and
daymares

suddenly enflesh.
A seismic shrug, a planet shudders
beneath alien stride.
He has arrived--with
inter(species)course.
Or rape.

earth, receive thy new possessor

THE LAST PASTORAL

Come live with me and be my love,
And we will all the pleasures prove
Damn Marlowe! and his pastoral!
Damn them both to bleakest hell

while I sit here listening
to that damned tape-deck malfunctioning,
squawking an incessant tape
of Renaissance poetry. Whatever ape

programmed that racket should be shot.
No . . . the idiot's already got
his reward, along with . . . . Damn
them all! This red button would ram

a warhead down their throats, if they
had throats again. They don't. I play
that incessant sing-song insane voice
for noise, you see. I have no choice

since Newman died. The bastard! Leaving
me alone like that. "Grieving
for Earth," he said he was. Like Hell!
For a ball of shit that might as well

blow itself to bits, explode
like a scarlet weed, unload
enough energy to bring
us home a million times. Sing,

damn you! Come live with me or die
like Newman. Hell, I didn't lie
to him, or seduce him while
we were drunk that night. I'll

admit that we were bombed--bad pun,
I know--we were drunk then . . . none
too sober, not sober enough
to want to see that dirty scuff

that hid the stars, dirty smudges
of a planet that turned its grudges
on itself--yeah, we were drunk,
two breathing bodies encased in a hunk

58

of lifeless metal on an airless moon.
We talked and cried and cursed and soon--
oh what the bloody hell!--we touched,
broke some convention much

more "honored in the breach" than valid
for two dead men in the pallid
ash light of dead earth. **If all
the world and love were young** like gall

or salt in slashes the tape mewed
piously. And we were nude,
bodies alive and warm where had been
only death before. **And truth in**

every shepherd´s tongue I took
him. When we woke, he looked
at me. He stood there naked, bare
and skinny, silent. He bled stale air

into the lock and stared at me.
And cried, damn him! He cried! To see
his face like the ruined earth
gashed with lines, giving birth

to death . . . . He smiled once to mock
me, walked into the waiting lock,
sealed the hatch and decompressed
himself. His blood **But could youth last**

and love still breed and blood still bleed
exploding like a scarlet weed
against grey steel. **Had joys no date
nor age no need** His bloody hate

abandoned me! But I can get
him. I´ll show them, teach them yet
to fuck with me to shoot me
into empty space **If we**

had worlds enough and leave me here
alone **and time and time** they´ll fear
me. Damn that tape **and time and time**
This coyness laddie were no crime

were no shut it off! **crime**
no crime My warhead´s poised, primed

59

aimed.   I´ll blast the earth to bits--
no, I can´t--it´s gone.   Hit

the button anyway! Maybe
Deserts of vast eternitie
it´ll short-circuit, explode
itself like a scarlet weed, unload

its flames . . . . Newman!   Where´s he gone?
Get in here, you shit--don´t leave me alone!   .
·Then these delights my mind might move
To live with thee and be

THE SHEEP IN PEWS

"The hungry sheep look up, and are not fed . . . ."

--John Milton, "Lycidas"

"It was the archetype of nightmare: trapped, incapable of moving, with monstrous menacing beasts edging closer."

--John Brunner, The Sheep Look Up

The sheep in pews
look up as the shepherd bleats
and do not understand good news
nor cultivate good seeds
but grow rank weeds

because they are not sheep.
They graze on asphalt fields,
wander concrete trails through deep
sky-scraping forests of steel
structures, sealed

in metal alloy cars.
And parables of sheep and shepherds, tales
of village greens and kingdoms far
away in space and time--such fail
and in pale

twilight they wander, sheep no more,
crying for new parables of steel and brick,
hungry with a hollowness like a dead reactor's
        core,
fearing to become like devils sick
with sin--they eat slick
words and pain for more.

SONATA ENIGMATA

Sometimes the gaping maw
double-rowed teeth
unsheathed
and ivory white
frightens me. Is it
grimacing at my pretensions,
subverting my joys

or smiling skull-tight

waiting to consume me
with sound,
chew me thoroughly
and spit out just the hull
of me
when the music
dies

MIGRATION

Tule fog tucks the hillsides,
A damp quilt over sleeping soil
Near Highway 5. Click--Click
Metallic on crumbling concrete.
Click--Click. Reverberating
From every side. Click--Click
   Eastward, beyond the rusting wreckage
Of a tank, a phantom glint of gold.
A unicorn, golden-horned,
Milk-fleshed and ghostly; its horn
Probes corruptive air.
One hoof scrapes decomposing
Asphalt slick with
Deadly moisture,
Wraithy in a world of wrath.
Behind, silent as breath, they come:
Small ones first--a basilisk,
Darting dampened eyes. Nearby
A salamander puffs orange
Smoke--its flames have died. A troll,
Manticora, and chimera,
Harpy winging low, almost
Aground. And a dragon, invisible
Nearly. Sphinx and griffin. Then none.
No more shadows in the fog.
   The unicorn stands alone
By the roadway. For a breath
It waits while silence wraps
The earth. Its gold glows and dims;
It turns and fades
Among fruitless furrows.
   Decaying in the darkness lies
A vaguely human form,
Grey-fleshed and lesion-haunted--
The last imagination dies
In irradiated air.
Westward the eerie glow of
Final twilight. The unicorn looks back
Once . . . . . And disappears.

ALIEN VISTAS

I. Surf

A cosmic storm
somewhere   out there

And green-bronze beaches
sliiide themselves
beneath curling waves

II. Reptilia

        cold lifeless
        scales of sloughed-off skin
twine
redundant
through hollowness
and
        sinuous pre-dawn chill--
cold-bloody remnants
of a body
                itching and new nude
atavistically struggling
to re-enter a skin
                        too small
                        outgrown
                        painfully
tight.

III. First Contact

Like swallows--forgotten avians
on a planet long forgotten

Chwrth mud-daub beneath wide flange-eaves
snuggled in cool shadows
high above reflecting glinting
white crystalline pillars.
Nest piled on nest--
brown hirsute nests,
single-level condominiums on

prime beach-front property.
Swivel-necked, Chwrth peer unblinkingly
toward the glassy ocean arching
bow-taut
north and south--
toward the blue-green band
defining the lens´s furthest boundary,
and the alien-silver needle skyward thrusting.

Hunch-shouldered, tail-braced,
Chwrth perch on vertical walls.

How do they stay up there,
and not even suction cups
on their feet?

IV. Aube

Cruel sun! How soon--too soon you slither
amber-rimed glass, rose-dusted sills, then down
thick-red-blood carpeting. He turns
in sleep, my midnight lover turns, and through thin
        walls
the other clumsily begins his morning rituals.

Officious fool--warden of unending days!
He does not guess--would not believe it if he
        could.
But still, ssssh . . . . A knife-edged sunray
        slices
sheening counterpanes, caressing bed, slashing
        flesh
with hideous warmth. And my lover moans.

Gods (if ever gods there be)
not again! Don´t leave me alone in this dawn,
condemned to share a daylight bed
with the old one creaking wearily beyond the wall.
Sunlight, higher now, cuts ebony coverlets:
he wanes in agony--o **gods! why can I not awaken him**
before . . . .

Darkness takes him once again;
diurnal sunrise stabs my lover´s fading breast,
sullen emptiness mocks me from my bed.

V. The Essence of the ´Other´

Mounds of packed brown sugar
carmelized
               carbon-blackened
               bitter and crisped--
Hills
shiver in aureal twilight
as harvest-breath
       insinuates waist-high chinquapin
       and dusty scrub oak
migrates north
herding
          skittish leaves
          like unresponsive cattle--
          they spiral
          point to point
          and slip
                    nervously
          across quicksilver asphalt
          slick with oily residue

Within an hour
clouds cumulate
subtly shaping
          shadowing
New Worlds from Old.

FIFTH MOVEMENT AND FINAL:
Symphony in E-minor, "From the New Worlds"
(Organ Transcription)

The organ shudders--its console cramps beneath
Twisted wires barbed by molten dripping flesh
Fencing with notes pinioned like mourning doves
On stuttering lines of fate

Cathedral-calm, after the storm-
Fires, ruby-fires through stone lattice
Windows, ruby over shivered glass
Futurity in shards on stone-bone floors.

And I play--Nemo in his madness
Dared not play as I, call down blue-glowing death
And flame upon his Nautilus-ship-world
Adrift beneath black seas of scarlet flame.

I play--ghosts cluster, choirs of ghosts swell
The nave--all birth, all death together--
And I play, orchestrating darkness
Swelling greatly like a cancer from the East.

Vermilion keys the music. Blood light
Oozes thick lubricant on thick ivory,
Sticky, atom-hot, breath-moist like cloying fog,
     drying
With each breath. The organ shudders, weeps blood.

Ghosts cluster, press, applaud
My final chord ultimate music penultimate.
                                    For I
Cannot stop--I, the last--and surge
Beyond captive notes, beyond darkness bile-

Black, beyond looming world-wreck, beyond white
Ash outlined in petulant pain . . . beyond to
     oneliness.
Fifth movement of a symphony uncomposed--
Climax thrusting into deepest darkness.

CRITICAL MASS

Biscuits crumble in an age-
stained tin--juice gone vinegar
choking and acid

The last

And then hunger and thirst
and death
beneath a fading sun
upon a fading world

I raise them up
and dash them down again
spilling and shattering and
cursing
loss
that leaves me here.

And I alone am left alive
to tell the tale.

COSMETIC SURGERY

From far enough away Earth
seems a woman´s face smiling
at her paramour the moon.

She tucks her chin, hmmmming here and there,
preening in the mirror-sun, and frowns.
Those lines webbing her continents,

those blotches growing from river junctures--
age spots, perhaps, or (worse) some infectious
cancer threatening the treasure of her soil,

the clarity of turquoise seas.
She glances up. He is not watching.
So in the secrecy of night

glowing points like laser surgery
erase the lines, blot the blotches.
For a few long days (millenia apiece)

she hides her scars, her purpled bruises
beneath a silken silver veil,
her face averted from the stars.

Later, when the surgery has healed,
her skin lies smooth, unmarked, as once it was
when she was young. No lines,

no blotching at her rivers´ crescents.
Smiling, she turns her emptiness
to her paramour the moon.

Eternity has finally died--
of apathy or entropy or whatever

blackout skies emptier and deeper
than ever wait breathless

for the murmur of life
that will not return.

The sun retires, worn with
shinnying daily up the world´s

ash. He invites blue
giants and white dwarves to

Never-Land beyond the Galaxy.
They play pinochle and count

cribbage points in their retirement.
Moons and planets and satellites

queue for unemployment
benefits at the nearest

black hole, hoping for
positions in another

universe. Everything neat,
dusted, spotless, covered with black

linen emptiness. No memories
remain to haunt

with ectoplasmic perseverence
the hallways of eternity.

THE OTHER IN SHADOW

Fangs, scales, feathers, gills--
These I can handle,
These I can face;
Claws, screams from overgrown hills,
Beasts in the sunlight,
Lords of this place.

Creatures that hunt me, creatures that die,
Creatures like none
That exist on the Earth;
Creatures that run free, creatures that fly--
These I have hunted
And these show my worth.

But one Beast eludes me, and one terrifies--
The Other in Shadow,
The One that won't flee;
The One that stares back when I challenge its
    eyes--
The Other in Shadow,
And the Other is me.

Memento Mori

A petal wrapped in plasticine--
Yellow, crack-crazed with years,
It rests upon the starboard.
When I scan the monitor
To see byond my alloy womb
Into deeper space,
When I check the atmosphere,
Heat and oxygen and humidity
That keep me till my birth
At planetfall--
I see the petal.

It was my father´s.
I don´t know where he bought
(Or stole) it. But when he died
He handed it to me:
"This was Earth," he wheezed,
Breath struggling with breath in
Lungs burned black.
"This was Earth . . . the beauty
And the pride."
He thrust it to me,
Curled my fingertips around it
And died.

So now I watch stars float by--
Ghosts of stars hiding
In my monitors.
I look outward without end
And back,

When I let fall my gaze
On the petal aged to black,
Blood-red black,
The once-red petal of an Earthly rose.

AND SOFT AT SAMARKAND THE STONES

White world, wide world--
Wide with white beneath a startled star.

Seething heat, weaving heat--
Heat that weaves new-threaded elements
With spun-silk woof of once steel girders,
Crosswise on the warp of redwood strands.

Weaving fire, heaving fire,
White-hot fire against a yellow sun.

Time glows, stone flows,
Stretched into its patterned matrix-light.
White light, white night,
Cools to silent darkness and to ash.

VERBUM TERRAE

Earthworm burrow silt borings
clotted with mineral water

percolates like rich thick brown Colombian
dregs and grounds saturated

hardening like arteries squirming
through silt. In the beginning

and at the end Borings bearing
wormwords piecemeal through soil

read history in turns and swirls
of silt made stone--ephemeral

eternal-seeming now speaking
eloquences from long-dead silences

NAKED TO THE SUN (II)

I stand, the last, the past,
The present, the future locked

In sterile cells. Mutant eyes
Peer back across the Western wastes

Eastward to evening light, bright
Darkness dimming as I breathe

To blackness. Winds whisper
Generations to deaf ears,

Murmur broken hills: shells
Of silence coil serpent waves.

In the darkness life ends. Breath
Dies. Light decays. Silence.

Zenith high day breaks, quakes
Through roiling clouds to shine

On death, silence, stillness.
Naked to the sun

www.ingramcontent.com/pod-product-compliance
Lightning Source LLC
LaVergne TN
LVHW091207080426
835509LV00006B/871